BY THE SAME AUTHOR

Mirror Talk: a Memoir
Theatre Mad

Catbird

poems by

Barbara Alfaro

Finishing Line Press
Georgetown, Kentucky

Catbird

ACKNOWLEDGMENTS

The Blue Mountain Review: At Sea; Chasing After Midnight; Sea Fire
Boston Literary Magazine: Mourning Dove
The Chesapeake Reader: Afterlife
Glassworks: The Circumference of Something
The Journal of Kentucky Studies: Castle Cats
Minimus: A Child's Poem
New Millennium Writings: Oddly American
Poet Lore: Oddly American
Red Eft Review: Long Division
Remington Review: Image; Stolen Pearls
Silver: An Anthology of Poetry & Prose: In the Poem
Silver Birch Press: Riley & Lulu
Trouvaille Review: Ghazal; Snow Globe
Variant Literature: Even Indigo
Voices de la Luna: Catbird
WordWrights: Tough Guy; Jewels on Her Hat

Publisher: Leah Huete de Maines
Editor: Christen Kincaid
Cover Art: Michele Bulatovic, https://www.michelebulatovic.com/
Author Photo: Barbara Alfaro
Cover Design: Elizabeth Maines McCleavy

Order online: www.finishinglinepress.com
also available on amazon.com

Author inquiries and mail orders:
Finishing Line Press
P. O. Box 1626
Georgetown, Kentucky 40324
U. S. A.

Table of Contents

For Victor

Oddly American

In McDonald's this afternoon a punch
drunk fighter with a squashed face
shared a table with a woman
perhaps in her late fifties.
She was wearing button earrings,
a white blouse, blue skirt,
perfectly polished shoes,
her Lord & Taylor shopping bag
nestled beside her with its single rose.
The fighter wore dark clothes,
and spoke constantly.
His voice sounded scraped, raw,
and it was difficult for me
to listen to him without wincing.

Sometimes the woman looked away
but only for a moment, then
rested her chin on her joined hands
and leaned forward toward him
the way listening women do.
She looked like actresses
in old movies, ladylike,
lovely, and oddly American.
The fighter's face had been hurt
so often and so brutally
he no longer resembled himself.
Perhaps once he looked like Vinnie Love,
a boxer I knew when I was sixteen,
his face so beautiful I couldn't believe
he wanted to be a fighter.

Vinnie took me to a party.
Most of the people were drunk.
An older man, a writer,
beckoned me to join him
in another room. I followed him.
The light was turned out.

He slid his hands along my legs.
The door opened. Vinnie switched
on the light and began
punching the writer.

Later, voices, and the writer asking
that the light be turned off. And while
the fighter in McDonald's is talking,
at another table a baby is mangling
a handful of French fries.
I'm remembering my dress,
at home — so much blood,
I threw it away.
When Vinnie called in the morning,
I didn't want to talk,
didn't want to hear his voice.
I spoke but only pretended to listen.

Today I'm thinking of how
the angels fought. They had no wings
but moved as quickly as thought.
They never used their hands
but stunned and kept enemies from them
with sound, the way whales do.
In other occasions, they playfully made
garlands of breath-whispers humans
could not see but felt brushing tenderly.

What did his voice sound like
before it was wounded — liquid, sure?
Did he have a New York accent
or sound vaguely foreign
as sons of immigrants sometimes do?
Which pounding caused what would never heal?

The woman from Lord & Taylor
did not reach over and touch
the fighter's hand but I wanted her to.

Once

We were all so slim and lovely
and certain of our dreams.
It was grand.
We were grand.
Grand.

Moving Day

A snake curled toward me
as I opened the front door.
My husband said,
"You're in Kentucky."
We have no snakes
in New York City.
We have roaches, rats,
& politicians but
we have no snakes
in New York City.
Manhattan has the Met,
the Mets, and Broadway.
It has no snakes except
the few at the zoo.
Dream symbolism says
the serpent is a star ~
signaling good fortune,
swell sex, and more.
Shining in dreams,
sliding through lawns,
there are always snakes
somewhere it seems.

Chasing After Midnight

For Arsenio Alfaro

A cricket the nurses were chasing
after midnight seemed to amuse
the professor of languages
who told his wife in the morning
he'd been serenaded by an insect.

Strapped to the bed because of
attempts to get away,
he confounded the staff
by speaking different languages
loudly without restraint
as if in a stark Pentecost.

Snow Globe

Angel in a glass sphere, all
who touch you hold your destiny.
A movement of a single hand
and fake snow covers you.

On your pedestal of hidden music
you cannot see a kiss, stars,
the tree cut from the forest
Christmas Eve.

Imagine the crystal breaking,
liquid spilling, wings dissolving
as you become large and human.

Still
        alone
                you breathe

The Circumference of Something

There we are, lying on the soft carpet,
me child-size, you a young woman,
pedaling invisible, nonexistent
bicycle wheels imagined in the air.

You, who held me too tightly
and loved lilacs, told me the boy
next door would never ask me out
if I kept beating him at basketball.

Years later, I hocked my wedding band
rather than borrow again. Mother,
why is it I see the screened door
and your silhouette but not your face
when you call me in from play?

Tough Guy

For Henry Brautigan

The Brooklyn apartment on Fenimore St.
had high ceilings and arched doorways.
After supper, in her favorite chair,
Mama read the comics to my brother.
I was at the dining table with you,
a sketchbook, charcoals, and pastels.
You taught me how to draw pictures
of a tree, a man's face, a rowboat near a lake.
Quiet as a lamb, I almost never spoke
when near you. Seven, skinny,
and sinless as a jellyfish,
I was silly with the mystery of childhood.
Still, Papa, somehow you conveyed to me
quiet is where you go to get soul things out.

There is a photograph of you, looking serious
in your soldier's uniform. My mother said
you were a "tough guy." You came home
"sailing" and told my grandmother,
"I was gonna knock his block off
but I'd see your face, Annie."
This seems odd to me as I only knew
the old gentleman — impeccably dressed,
manicured nails, a perfectly tended mustache.
Once, at Thanksgiving time, you won a live turkey,
came home, put it in the bathtub, and went to bed.
Eighty-two now, my mother laughs when she tells
how that turkey nearly scared her to death.

Coney Island night noises, crowds, and rides
surround you as you survey the boardwalk,
the rollercoaster, a giant doodle against the sky.
Couples walk along the edge of the water,
barefoot and hungry but too moonstruck
to leave the beach and eat hot dogs at Nathan's.

Summer just beginning and only a tough guy
could let the memory of that winter morning
come full force again. There was a blizzard
so you delivered your own and only son.
Stillborn, you placed his silent body
on a pillow and wept while your Annie
whispered your name as if it were a prayer.

Today, at church, the children put on a pageant
celebrating the Three Kings and the Epiphany.
Baby Jesus was a girl. No one seemed to mind.
Last year a Guatemalan baby named Juan,
in this country for surgery, played Jesus.
Several months after his return to Guatemala,
he died of cholera. This Guatemalan Jesus
is in some way connected to my dead infant uncle.

How quiet it was fishing from the rowboat with Papa,
early in the morning, how quiet and how green.
How quiet it was, after supper, at the table,
watching Papa place his pastels gently in their box.

Carnival Music

When I was a girl
the square shaped man who ran
a ferris wheel
let me ride free.

The square shaped man who ran
from his mother to me
let me ride free.
I giggled inside the circle.

From his mother to me,
love was a hallucination.
I giggled inside the circle.
I knew nothing.

Love was a hallucination,
a ferris wheel.
I knew nothing
when I was a girl.

Slippers

My father's bedroom slippers had labels
that glowed in the dark, rectangles
in the instep of each slipper. At night
he placed his slippers beside the double bed
shared with my mother. As a child,
suffering from nightmares,
I'd wake in the middle of the night,
tiptoe like a burglar through the house,
to see those two glowing patches guiding
me to my father's side of the bed where
I'd curl on the floor, a furtive thing.
We stayed overnight at the house of new friends.
I heard my mother wonder
if I would be able to find them
in this strange house. After
I woke from the bad dream, I fell
before I found the room with the glowing
slippers and my parents breathing
strongly in the dark.

Riley & Lulu

What's your dog's name asked a boy of a woman and not waiting her reply continued My dog's name is Riley My dog's name is Lulu said the woman just then Riley a red dog reminiscent of Irish setters and German shepherds and other miscellaneous breeds and Lulu a beige dog of even more dubious lineage than Riley interrupted their afternoon swim in the model boat pond to shake-splash their owners a portable radio a pair of shoes and me They swam again then galloped and chased on the wet concrete Lulu doing most of the chasing with the grassy abandon city dogs on park days know making strangers laugh out loud and now intimidated by the sailors who were not laughing these handmade or purchased boats cost four hundred dollars baby and the pond is after all for them not Riley and Lulu the older brother of the boy attaches a leash to Riley's collar and the woman bribes Lulu into a semblance of quietude with pets and scratches but mind you Lulu and Riley are eyeing each other all this time they're approximately five feet away from one another and What's this Oh no a beagle well a partial beagle bouncing into the pond a stick between his teeth guarded as though it were the golden fleece and Lulu that hussy swimming after his neat patched little body as though absolutely nothing has happened between her and Riley for God's sake chained and barking in pain while a bumble bee is bugging pun intended me and a little girl lopes by announcing Now my other front tooth is crooked!

Untitled

Ethel Lang was the most beautiful girl
in Saint Anastasia Grammar School.
Tall and graceful, she usually wore
a sprig of tiny flowers in her hair,
lilies-of-the-valley or violets, fastened
with a tortoise shell barrette. Winters,
a jeweled butterfly took their resting place.

When Ethel entered a classroom,
a message for the teacher in her hand,
even second-graders knew to look.
Some never saw her eyes or heard
her voice and so she seemed to them
almost an apparition of some catholic sort.

It would be terrible to think she
met some sad and wholly unfair fate.
Eerie hells await even the beautiful.
Rather, imagine her arranging flowers,
loosely, so they breathe. She is
laughing easily at a friend's remark.
In another room of the house
guests from other countries gather,
the scent of jasmine everywhere.

K Street

On K Street, in Washington,
a woman in a designer suit
adjusts a hat selected
from a table of many hats.
The street peddler holds
a mirror before her
as demonstrators chant
"Long Live Freedom!"
Some people, on their lunch hour,
pause to watch the marchers
while the woman considering
the purchase of a hat,
pinches the wool of another hat
with her perfectly manicured hand.

Fur Coat

For Irene Smith

My mother owned a fur coat,
Persian Lamb, black and curly.
I still see her smiling as she looped
its soft collar around her neck.
That coat was her one connection
to those without money worries.
No small thing for a woman
who taught four children to say,
"The lady of the house is not at home"
whenever creditors called. She signed
Christmas and birthday cards
"Always," "Irene" or "Mom."

Months before dying, Mother
liked to use the coat as an extra
blanket even though it smelled
of perspiration and of sickness.
In movie death scenes, the room
is always immaculate, with perfectly
arranged flowers, closeups of caring.
There are no scattered Kleenex tissues,
smelly old fur coats, or seventy pound
women shouting, "Take me home Jesus!"
The lady of the house is at home now and
Always,

La Bella

For Isolina Alfaro

This is the time, during the war,
la bella started wearing rainbow dresses.

To some they looked like ordinary clothing
but to those who loved, the dresses

contained all the colors of the rainbow.
When the beautiful one was a child

she thought she could
touch the stars from a hilltop
and they would feel sharp and warm.

A Child's Poem

In second grade, I wrote a poem about God.
I compared Him to an old sea captain
who looked not surprisingly like Santa Claus.
I put the words in bunches of four lines.

The next day my teacher read the poem,
told me she knew very well I had not written it.
I was in my twenties before I wrote another,
locked in a marriage to a man who loved sailing.
We lived in a house by the bay but even the grey
water and orange sun could not calm our union.

I would sit in a gold chair and write poems
till there was nothing in me but the desire
for sleep. A cat that I loved very much
befriended a chubby, speckled rabbit.
The two would walk along the water's edge
unaware that they were natural enemies.

Once in a restaurant I heard a man describe deer hunting.
"You choose the one you want most and then kill it."
I repeated the line as if it contained some secret.
I repeated the line so I would not forget it.

Jewels on Her Hat

Emeralds, rubies,
amethysts, all glass, the size
of quarters on her felt hat,
sprinkled like blessings.
Round and proud, the old
woman took the seat
reserved for seniors
and those with disabilities.
Brass buttons nestled
near the gems, humble
and unlike the large
jewels that announced
their peculiar grace.

Castle Cats

On the stone steps near the kitchen,
above the grotto, a trio of grey cats
snuggle in the smell of what cook
is preparing for guests. Nearby,
a striped kitten sits undecided
while a slim black cat
jumps beside a rose bush.
Rubbing, purring and roaming,
similar cats conspire in the courtyard.
Mousers, each one of them,
felines, efficient at killing —
affectionate, sensual, warm,
enjoying the Tuscan sun.

Kept

Donatello's "The Lion" is cordoned off from viewers in the National Museum of the Bargello, Florence.

Kept from touch
in some intuitive move,
straight on your stone pedestal
in the Donatello Room.

In some intuitive move,
before your gray mane and eyes,
in the Donatello Room,
as if you miss the sculptor's hands.

Before your gray mane and eyes,
easy in forgotten grace,
as if you miss the sculptor's hands
or feel them still in stillness.

Easy in forgotten grace,
straight on your stone pedestal,
as if you miss the sculptor's hands
kept from touch.

Ghazal

On the edge of the witches' well in the garden,
angels breathe their summer spell in the garden.

A child's voice insists something to his mother.
Suddenly, the sound of bells in the garden.

Celebration bells! Insistent like the boy.
Luscious noise and joy swell in the garden.

Honeysuckle sorrow left at home, Barbara,
Whose secrets will you share, tell in the garden?

Bedtime Stories

September 2001

Long ago and far away,
you are the sleepy boy, listening
to stories of girls and ghosts
while outside, trees tremble
in the vast, unforgiving night.

Somewhere there are people burning books.

Seven and wearing ski pajamas,
weary and sincere, you ask
for just one more story.
Remember walking in the woods,
like fairytale children,
pausing by a pond
to watch mallards glide,
scooping toads in our hands,
laughing as they jump aside.

Somewhere there are people burning books.

In the morning, a list that begins
"Bottled water, peanut butter, duct tape"
changes to the first draft of a poem.
Here, in a suburb of Washington,
I sleep and wake to the great grumbling
sound of fighter aircraft as if the skies are hungry.

Brother, once upon a time America…

Sleigh Bed

Visiting Emily Dickinson's home in Amherst, Massachusetts

After days divided into increments
of grocery lists, poetry, and baking bread,
weary and delighted, you slip into
your dark wood single bed
and feel soft linens against your skin.

Did you exchange hungry kisses
with Judge Otis P. Lord on that bed
or was it sacred space where
only dreams and poems were wed?

Harvard looted everything of yours
except this sleigh bed,
its head and foot boards slanting outward,
where you lay listening and let
the hodgepodge of eternity in.

First Kiss

Teddy O'Connor, I dreamed of you last night.
You were the age you would be now
and still handsome in your quiet way.

Remember us, in our Easter Sunday best,
beside my father's mint green Chevrolet,
holding torch-shaped ice cream cones.

Ten years later, I'm wearing a prom dress.
You are Cary Grant in a rented tux.
You broke my heart that night,
being too attentive to another.

Somewhere between the Carvels
and senior prom, probably
when we were twelve, we paused
in a Long Island woods and
sat beside each other on a fallen tree.
You surprised me with a kiss
and I fell silent as a log.

In the dream, you said you live in Delaware.
I wonder how you are now.
The fool part of me is tempted to see
how many Theodore O'Connors
live in Wilmington but if I found you,
what could I say?

Teddy O'Connor, I dreamed of you last night.

Afterlife

People do odd things
after the death of a parent —
lose their faith,
end a marriage,
travel somewhere
they read of long ago,
as if, as if…
the faces they owned
before they saw
the things no one tells,
would somehow return,
certain and vaguely young.

The last time I saw my mother
she winked at me when encouraged
to attend a sing-along.
I understood that wink to mean
there wasn't much to sing about
stationed by the large window,
in a locked wheelchair, so the nursing
home staff could move freely.
That window waits for me.

It does no one good
to cry in the dark,
"I was wrong." You need
to go on in the way
almost sleeping children
pull bedcovers and sigh
into the breadth of night.

In the Poem

For Victor

I remember you in your red robe,
standing in a triangle of sunlight
as you feed our cats, put coffee on,
& break bread into pieces for the birds
outside in the snow. You give me a poem
you have written. In the poem, what is best
in me is exaggerated, the way truths are
in dreams and reading it, I see our love.

Also

"And when he has found it, he lays it upon his shoulders, rejoicing."
Luke: 15:5

Trembling
when the shepherd found you,
touched you, calmed you,
made your breath like music,
lifting you to his shoulders,
you nuzzled his face,
a laugh spurted from him
and he said, "I am glad also."

Supper

They smell of fish and sunlight.
Peter always laughs the loudest,
quiet John is a favorite of the Lord.

The evening is heavy with the perfume
of desert flowers and the scarred moon,
a perfect circle.

Clearing his throat,
the nervous disciple
rises from the table,
careful not to spill the wine.

Heart

I sold my heart today,
the gold locket I seldom wore &
my grandfather's cufflinks,
in a mall jewelry store.

The gold locket I seldom wore &
purchased at Christmas,
my grandfather's cufflinks,
melting after the teller's remark.

Purchased at Christmas,
these shining things,
melting after the teller's remark,
"Good for you, you've made

yourself a little money."
My grandfather's cufflinks,
shining, engraved.
I sold my heart today.

Spinning

You can let your sadness show
in laundromats and Walmart stores.
There are no paparazzi for the poor.
A mother folds faded towels.

In laundromats and Walmart stores,
a girl draws bears wearing hats.
A mother folds faded towels,
all the while wondering.

A girl draws bears wearing hats,
the way one sees in movies,
all the while wondering
when the spinning ends.

The way one sees in movies,
silvery dark,
when the spinning ends.
Once she dreamed of dancing.

Silvery Dark,
there are no paparazzi for the poor.
Once she dreamed of dancing.
You can let your sadness show.

The Rocking Chair

In the nursery the ghost of a boy stands
on a rocking chair, holding its back.
A miniature prisoner of wood,
looking through its slats.
He misses the crazy little dog
who barks at the toaster, his tomboy
sister, and toasted cheese sandwiches.

"I don't know why you insist on keeping
that rocker," the father said. "As far
as I'm concerned, it's like honoring
a murder weapon." The eyes of the boy's
mother move slightly, her only reply.

Gentle prayers dance in the air like a child
blowing bubbles through a circle on a stem.

The boy kisses the faces of his sister
and mother, touches his father's hand.

And now he is with me his First Mother…

Before Dark

"Home before dark," our mother's voice
trails after my brother and me like a kite tail
as we scamper to stickball. Sundown
happens too soon so we run to the blue
house as if our lives depend on time.
After supper, in the hallway, I hear
"She's got to stop following me around"
and imagine his pals poking fun at
a skinny kid sister tagging along.

Today, I can't help it, I'm happy.
God knows why.
I'm holding on to heaven.
If I let go, what's there? Nothing
but memory and pain.
I confess I've been unfaithful
to my dreams and my stories,
leaving them alone and unwritten
in the distant shimmering house,
the house they burst forward from,
rushing and true. I have to keep writing.
That's how it is, before dark…

Ghosts of Dublin Castle

Whistlin' or singin'
is how we are told to enter
the great hall when carryin'
trays of food so the grand guests
hear us comin' an' can change
the subject of their conversation
if 'tis politics or a bit of gossip
and sure, ye cannot swallow
a wee bite of food while ye are
whistlin' or singin' …

At Sea

For Celia Sheridan

*On a voyage from Ireland to America, my great grandmother
died giving birth to her son, who also died.*

Your husband holds your daughter's hand
as he mumbles something about heaven,
angels very near them both, still,
listening, like sailors on watch.

I imagine you slender, with long hair,
laughing softly, even when so ill.
That is the silly thing we are taught,
to be brave instead of sad.
Were you a devout Catholic
or did you read the Tarot,
trembling when the death card turned?

Your gentleness which I am
suddenly certain of is like
a white rose in a clear vase.
I like to think you owned
at least one beautiful dress,
a girl's princess dress,
soft, lace, and so feminine
those who saw you smiled.

I wish I had a photograph of you
in that perfect dress, young,
Irish, and susceptible to dreams -

long before the waves
rocking the coffin ship
like a cradle in the sea.

Ghost Girl

In a concert hall with eleven
chandeliers, four clever musicians
play, as the ghost of a girl
pops through an invisible loop,
swims in the air, her sheer white
gown easy and comfortable.

Pausing, turning upright,
she holds a huge glass tier
in the way a subway rider
holds on to a strap, her small
incandescent feet dangling
like notes on a vast page.

1928

Edwina, nicknamed "Beanie"
because she was so tiny,
took the Staten Island Ferry one
morning and for the price of a nickel,
began her death.

In her imagination, she stood on deck,
mounted the railing as if
it were a thin horse, and let go.
But it wasn't like that at all.
So much easier to slip through
one of the triangles of space
in the chain gate at the stern of the ship.

For weeks she fretted about
her gold cross and pearl ring
but it came to her in a flash,
during one of her bouts of insomnia,
the idea of wrapping them in a handkerchief
and putting both in the poor box at church.

There was no evil urging voice
or montage of her life the way
one reads in novels and magazines,
only an image of a beautiful infant face,
beaming and glad, before the icy splash.

It was the year Amelia Earhart
was the first woman to fly
across the Atlantic,
Eugene O'Neill received the Pulitzer Prize,
and "Am I Blue?" and "Crazy Rhythm"
were favorite songs.

I always understand suicides,
my poet bones snapping
in remembrance.

The Wood House

"Let's not go," I said that Sunday
we were working on the boat.
The priest had dentures that
clicked when he talked and his
sermons were as boring as sand.

It's so easy for saints.
They love God ferociously,
don't even feel the flame
of ordinary lives. But we do,
we do.

I remember the exact address,
long porch, indifferent sunrises,
and wondering what the police
emergency squad would think
if a suicide left the supper dishes
undone.

Gun Owner

He shot every lightbulb in the house when I left him.
For a long time, I must have believed his threat.
Why didn't I make a run for it? At least, try.
Laughing, he said he wasn't going to hit me again.

For a long time, I must have believed his threat —
"If you ever love anyone, I'll kill you!"
Laughing, he said he wasn't going to hit me again.
We used to hold hands on the way to church.

"If you ever love anyone, I'll kill you!"
I remember his words but not his voice.
We used to hold hands on the way to church.
He shot every lightbulb in the house when I left him.

Reflection

For Anna Brautigan

In a distance made safe by light
I see you before your mirror
spin your hair into a circle
carefully, with warm precision

as though such tasks were luxury.
Wrapping and fastening your hair
with large hairpins shaped like A's,
you tilt your head gently right then

left, catching a stray strand
you place a final hairpin and
turning to me smile easily
across the decades of your death.

Even Indigo

The Lovers card in the Tarot has all
the colors of a rainbow, even indigo.
Raphael, winged and unsmiling,
blesses a naked woman and man.

You brought the battered woman
to my dorm room as if it were
some sort of shelter for the sad.
Listening, I memorize your face.

I could not stand near you, or
the middle-aged English prof,
yes, him, without knowing
what others must feel often.

Augustine tells when you speak
a sentence one word must die
before the next word is born.
I kept ghosts of former loves too long.

Tree Life

Trees amaze me most in winter when
stark against slate skies
slim, long branches bend. In December
snow somehow gently clings.
Pagans danced around oaks, in awe.
Trees were holy things.
Squirrels hurry as sparrows startle
through large, breathing limbs,
squeaking speckled, easy hymns.
Pale, crisp leaves lay soft nearby,
in winter when trees amaze me most.

Mourning Dove

"The doves are here!" I'd yell
to my husband in another room
as if weekend guests had just arrived.
Something about their quirky
elegance always got to me.

Visiting our wood deck often,
inculcating warmth in the sadness
of their sound, bobbing, preening,
grooming one another with caring pecks,
they seemed in every way a perfect couple.

One morning there was only one.
Had the partner died from some disease
I don't know the name of —
or a hunter's bullet? Like a fool,
I whispered a prayer. For weeks,
I saw the dove, then not again.

I don't know if that prayer was for the dove
or me. Familiar with the strength of omens,
I know how cruel even soft gray ones can be.

Catbird

It began with the catbird lying in the lawn —
screechy cries and failed attempts to fly.
I stroked its back before it trembled twice
and died. At this time, I had a small role
in a film, a character described
as "a bit of a playgirl, a real catbird."

At three a.m., I am awakened by loud music
on the transistor radio your mother holds
beside her as if she believes noise, idiotic
or lovely, keeps death away. I loved her once
when I saw her lipstick hidden under the pillow.
Like Marlene Dietrich in "Dishonored,"
applying lipstick before the firing squad,
no pale mouth would greet eternity.

Some, dying, scream at those caring for them.
Others are so gentle, hospice staff fall in love
with them. Your father was like that. My mother
was another, telling jokes even near the end.
Irish people are a little crazy that way.

And you, my heart,
you never complained.
Not once.
Cancer.
I wish there were a way
to spit that word rather than say it.

I see the catbird's bead black eyes
before I sleep and dream forgotten things.

Beware of Old Photographs

I'm surprised at how pretty I once was
but not at your gentleness you held in your
sixties and your sickness our smiles and
unembarrassed love recorded through
the decades in coated color startled by
my sharp cry I cover your photograph
with my hand to hold what the memory
the pain the knowledge from me defeated
I close the album stage four cancer sounds
theatrical I have no photographs of it
only holograms of horror and of holiness.

Transitioning

For Lucas

"The doctors call it transitioning," your mother tells me.
"Some infants don't cry when they come from the womb
to the room and he wouldn't so he had to be put on oxygen."
She kisses your forehead and pats your side.

Born early, you charm all in the budget hair cuttery.
If one believes in paradise, it's easy to imagine
angelic reluctance to your transition to a dark stroller
and fleece blue blanket crazy with windmills.

People always say "precious" when they
see an infant but damn, you really are adorable.
You, Lucas, in your striped pj's and bib with polka dots,
you, Lucas, happy and gurgling, make my eyes glisten.

Image

After all these decades,
I still see you across
the lunch counter,
your left hand holding
a napkin loosely before
your lips, your right hand
spooning ice cream into
your hidden mouth. I stare
downward as if my sandwich
were fascinating and un-
intentionally raise my eyes
the second the cloth falls,
your nervous toothless smile
piercing me even now.

Enchantment

In fairytales, enchantment means
bewitchment...
a man turned into a beast,
a girl asleep a hundred years,
both redeemed by a shining kiss.

Another meaning
of enchantment is enrapture,
a universe I imagine where
evil is not allowed
and the music of intelligence is heard
even while one sleeps.

Aurora

Am I so far from my own beauty
the rich dreams will not come

but in their place, nightmares
of knives and noise.

My gown is so heavy in the summers.
If only I could pull it from me.

Who have I harmed that I
may never know my name?

Mother Gothel

How mean sweet people can be.
Listen to me, Rapunzel.
Your father is a thief who stole
from my garden, and his wife,
a woman who gave you away.
The world is an evil place.
Trust only me. I would rather
you be locked in a tower
than broken by a man.
Come, sit beside me where
I can see you and touch your hair.

Stolen Pearls

To the night swollen with wonder
a girl whispers a prayer.
Afraid the clasp might break,
she hides a strand of pearls in her cape.

A girl whispers a prayer.
Under tiered chandeliers,
she hides a strand of pearls in her cape.
Breathless, excited, uncertain,

under tiered chandeliers
nine couples dance.
Breathless, excited, uncertain,
a thief crosses the floor.

Nine couples dance.
Lifting the pearls,
a thief crosses the floor.
She turns from a mirror.

Lifting the pearls,
cool in her warm hand,
she turns from a mirror
to the night swollen with wonder.

Questions

What thoughts did Psyche know
tied to that tree? Were memories soft
as snow flurries or piercing like an arrow

rushing through her when the west wind
freed and carried her to love? Did she faint
from fear and dream of sleeping butterflies

hiding somewhere in the dark?
Is the goddess happy now, winged,
and occasionally petitioned?

Don't Expect Love

Don't expect love.
Stay silent within
the remembrance of
those chilly evenings
right before summer
when you take out
the trash for the trucks
in the morning and the air
is cool and caressing
and you think to yourself
That is how the world tastes.

Long Division

For Sheridan Smith

I never told the first man in my life I loved him.
I never thanked him for helping me with math.

He could do long division in his head.
I never said how impressive it was that he

graduated from high school at fifteen or sad
the money he'd saved for college paid for

his brother's surgery. I doubt my grandmother,
an Irish immigrant, knew about scholarships.

I never thanked him for being the only one
who didn't judge me when I left my husband.

Four or five years old and curled on his lap,
I played possum and pretended to be asleep

because I knew when my mother said, "Sherry,
put her to bed," my father would always answer

"Not just yet, Irene, I don't want to disturb her."
I never told the first man in my life I loved him.

Sea Fire

Far from the shore and waves
in the deepest part of the sea

luminescent creatures swirl.
Clever beings

who never know the sun,
creating and owning light.

Dragonfish, catsharks, lanternfish,
others unnamed, battle or beckon

with glowing bodies ~
their quick movement

startling the water
like the surprise of joy.

BARBARA ALFARO is the recipient of a Maryland State Arts Council Individual Artist Award for her play *Dos Madres,* two Jenny McKean Moore writing scholarships at The George Washington University, and a Tenacious Women Scholarship from the Kentucky Women Writers Conference. A graduate of Goddard College and the American Academy of Dramatic Arts, she has acted in productions of Shakespeare in the Park at Woodland Park, the Actors Guild, and Lexington Children's Theatre in Lexington, Kentucky. Her poems and essays have appeared in various publications including *Poet Lore, The Blue Mountain Review* and *Glassworks.* She is the author of a full-length play, a collection of ten-minute plays, a collection of short stories, two children's stories, and a chapbook of poems. *Mirror Talk,* her memoir about working in theatre, won the IndieReader Discovery Award for Best Memoir. A widow, living in Lexington, Kentucky, she shares her days with a Maltese named Darby.

www.ingramcontent.com/pod-product-compliance
Lightning Source LLC
Chambersburg PA
CBHW021204090426
42740CB00008B/1221